April & May

by
Mark Nicholls

This first edition published in Australia in 2018 by:

Prahran Publishing
P.O. Box 2041, Prahran, Victoria, 3181

© Copyright Mark Nicholls 2018

Mark Nicholls has asserted his legal and moral right under the Copyright Act 1968 to be identified as the author of this work.

Published by arrangement with
Prahran Publishing, Australia.

All rights are strictly reserved.

No part of this publication may be reproduced, stored in a retrieval system or transmitted, in any form or by any other means, without the publisher's prior permission in writing. Copying of this script for performance reasons is also strictly prohibited by law, either in whole or excerpts from.

This book is sold subject to the condition that it shall not, by way of trade or otherwise, be lent, resold, hired out or otherwise circulated without the publisher's prior consent in any form of binding or cover other than that in which it is published and without similar condition, including this condition, being imposed on the subsequent purchaser.

Every reasonable effort has been made to trace copyright holders of material reproduced in this book, but if any have been inadvertently overlooked the publishers would be glad to hear from them. The story, all names, characters, and incidents portrayed in this book are fictitious. No identification with actual persons past or present, places, buildings, and products is intended or should be inferred.

ISBN 978-1-922263-00-1 Paperback
ISBN 978-1-922263-01-8 eBook

Dewey: 822.4

A catalogue record for this book is available from the National Library of Australia

Performance Licensing and Royalty Payments

Mark Nicholls retains control of both the amateur and professional stage performance rights of this play. No unauthorised performance should occur without the express and written permission of the playwright.

Restriction of Alteration

There shall be no modifications of any kind to the play including deletion of dialogue (including objectionable language), changes to characters gender or names, title of the play or music without the express and written permission from the author.

Sound and Video Recordings

This play may contain stage directions to include the use of music, video or other sound recordings either in part or in whole. The author and the publisher have not sought the right to use such content and performance rights permission should be obtained seperately. Permission to record audio and video recordings of all performances must also be explicitly given by the author in writing.

Author Credit

Performance rights approval requires credit be given to Mark Nicholls as the sole and exclusive author of the play. This obligation applies to the title page of every program or other advertising material distributed in connection to this play. The author's credit should appear immediately under the title of the play on all published material, and alongside no other individual. Font size of credit cannot be less than 50% of the largest letter used in the play's title.

Please email info@prahran.press
for all performance enquiries.

Dedication

for Madeleine Swain

"...the longer one lives the more one values you."
(GBS 1899)

About the Playwright

MARK NICHOLLS has been performing on various Melbourne stages since the age of six and has an extensive list of credits as a playwright, composer, singer, actor, producer and director. He is Senior Lecturer in Cinema Studies at the University of Melbourne where he has taught film since 1993.

He is the author of *Lost Objects of Desire: The Performances of Jeremy Irons* (2012), *Scorsese's Men: Melancholia and the Mob* (2004) and recently published articles on Italian Cinema, Powell and Pressburger's *The Red Shoes* and Sergei Diaghilev's celebrated company, The Ballets Russes.

Mark is a film critic and worked for many years on ABC Radio and for *The Age* newspaper, for which he wrote a weekly column between 2007 and 2009.

He lives in Melbourne with his partner, Ali Wirtz, and their two sons Oscar and Carlo.

Series Preface

I wrote these plays for only one reason, to perform them. I publish them here, therefore, somewhat reluctantly. They were never written to be read on the page by anyone but a treasured posy of performers that I trust to help me rescue them from the work. They were certainly never conceived of as anything so respectable as literature. Nevertheless, I have found two reasons to overcome my reluctance and my usual roguish prejudice against readers and writers in favour of performers and punters. One reason is that putting these plays into print provides the opportunity for the most engaged of those who saw and heard them to revive and revise the experience. The other reason is archival. I wish to leave a permanent, if inadequate, record of the facts of their production over a decade, in a private space in Melbourne, for the benefit of both a small, dedicated paying audience, and for a smaller band of compulsive show-folk.

Writing these plays for the talented actors, musicians and backstage characters whose creations are recorded here, and having the privilege of working with these artists to produce them, has been the most satisfying occupation of my otherwise horrendously charmed and fascinating life.

Now that they have had their blessed release in print, these plays are beyond the concern of any motivation I had to write them. Read them, o curious one, and work it out for yourself! One motivation I will record, however, rests in the inspiration generously given by those who worked on and attended these cosy performances, and so brought their privileged, fleeting moments of theatre securely into being.

About the Play

As is often the case for me, a piece of music, Chopin's Piano Concerto No. 2 in F Minor, Op. 21, haunted the writing of this play. We never used it in the production, but without it the play would not have been written in quite this way.

Some of the stimulus for my heroine, April, came from a telephone conversation with a woman I never met. This woman called me to provide a reference for one of my PhD students whom she was about to engage as a tutor for her "brilliant" son. If he was so "brilliant" I asked her, why did he need a tutor? Her reply I don't recall exactly, but it was about the same as if she were justifying the need for a Facebook account or twin basins in her en suite – "you've got to have it" was the sentiment.

Reading over them now, the attempts at verse here resound with unwittingly churlish tribute to English poet John Betjeman, who deserves better. The only song, 'Someday I'll Find a Boy...' is a pastiche of 'The Boy Next Door' and 'The Trolley Song' (Hugh Martin and Ralph Blane, 1944) and so is inevitably linked in my mind with Judy Garland sitting in the window in *Meet Me in St Louis* (Minnelli, 1944).

Unsatisfied desire threatens to overwhelm this play, but it is much more about friendship between women of different generations with similar problems and expectation of life. Our first experience of working with Grace Taylor and Luke Van Ryn, it stands clear in my mind as one of the most perfect rehearsal periods that I can remember. So, it is obviously as much about the pleasures of ensemble practice as about helicopter parents, earnest graduate students and the dilemmas posed by the options generation.

Characters

APRIL: a forty-something woman who is yet to make her move in life

LOUIS: a forty-two-year-old government official who has yet to make his move on April

JEREMY: a twenty-five-year-old student who spends all his time considering his next move

MAY: an eighteen-year-old high school graduate living with April, who is worried she may have to move

Conrad, April's husband, Teddy, April's son, and Carol, May's mother, are not seen on stage. In the case of the latter it is because she died ten years ago.

April and May was first performed at Rear 4, Clifton Hill, Victoria on the 17th of March 2010 with the following cast:

April:	Madeleine Swain
May:	Grace Taylor
Louis:	Mark Nicholls
Jeremy:	Luke Van Ryn
Directors:	Mark Nicholls
Associate Director:	Anika Ervin-Ward
Co-Producer:	Alison Wirtz

Scene One:

The play is set now, in early autumn, in an attentively decorated house in Kew, Victoria and a bar in Fitzroy. The action (or rather inaction) of the play takes place over two days. Throughout the play we can frequently hear a recording of the songs of Billie Holiday, or some equally melancholic chanteuse, playing in a distant room.

The scene opens on a veranda in APRIL's house. It is a warm autumn afternoon. APRIL and LOUIS are sitting on wicker chairs drinking wine. There is a small coffee table in front of them. APRIL is deep in the glossy magazine section of the Melbourne Age and LOUIS, although pretending to read the business section, is deep in thought. Neither of them is in any hurry to speak and it is some time before they do. These two know each other well and could sit all day without talking if required.

APRIL: It's still so warm for this time of the year. I told Jeremy he should stop coming at the end of the summer, but it doesn't seem to end.

LOUIS: It's nearly the middle of autumn. Anyway, who's Jeremy?

APRIL: I told you, Jeremy Brightwell. He's tutoring Teddy.

LOUIS: Do nine-year-olds really need tutoring? He seems to me to be terribly bright.

APRIL: Jeremy? He's a genius.

LOUIS: Teddy.

APRIL: Well he is. But it's all so competitive these days. You should see what goes on at these schools. They are impossible to get into and then if you want your kids to do well you have got to give them the extras. Some of them don't even have homework!

LOUIS: It's the end of civilisation! *[He takes a drink]* So do you mean poor Ted has had a tutor hanging around him all summer, flashing old masters in his face and demanding to know the population of Bogota?

APRIL: He's really good. He's fantastic with Teddy. It's amazing how much you can extend them if you get the right tutor.

LOUIS: Darling, he's nine. Can't you just let him have the summer off to run around and get into trouble?

APRIL: Oh, he's got plenty of time for that. Anyway, you don't know. You can't just let them wander the streets these days. There are some real weirdos out there.

Act 1 - Scene 1

LOUIS: Yeah, but with all the sport and the music and the bloody 'play dates' does he ever just get the chance to hang out and be bored? God, I used to waste the whole holidays watching cricket on TV and if the cricket wasn't on, I'd go out the back and play cricket.

APRIL: By yourself?

LOUIS: Yeah. Much better. In fact, if anyone asked me over to their place I would pretend I had strict parents who wouldn't let me go.

APRIL: I think you still do that a bit.

LOUIS: Never with you, my love.

APRIL: Anyway, he gets to run around at Portsea. We're a bit more relaxed there.

LOUIS: Two weeks without tutoring?

APRIL: No Jeremy came with us, but I told him to take it easy while we were there.

LOUIS: That sounds much more relaxing.

APRIL: Teddy loves Jeremy. It's like having a big brother. He's really more of a mentor for him than a tutor. Besides, we all like having someone else around. You know how depressing family Christmases can get? He's very funny, and he loves chatting. Even Conrad seems to have taken to him. They kept going off to play golf.

LOUIS: And I suppose May is not indifferent to having a cute post-grad on the premises?

APRIL: What do you mean?

LOUIS: You know what I mean.

APRIL: I don't think so. She's so young.

LOUIS: She's eighteen.

APRIL: No. May and her friends seem to be more interested in those boy band types. And they all look about twelve and a half! Jeremy is probably an old man to her, a bit too intellectual.

LOUIS: Is she going to keep living with you when she goes to uni?

APRIL: May?

LOUIS: Yeah.

APRIL: I don't see what other option she has. She doesn't have any money of her own. When Carol died, there was nothing left behind for May.

LOUIS: What about the father?

APRIL: Long gone. Whoever he was.

LOUIS: I didn't realise you and Conrad had been paying the bills all these years. That's very generous.

Act I - Scene I

APRIL: Sure. What could we do? She doesn't have anyone else. We can afford it. And I really love having her about, she so sweet, don't you think?

LOUIS: She's lovely. She's also very lucky.

The doorbell rings.

APRIL: That will be Jeremy now. You can meet him.

APRIL leaps up and leaves the room. LOUIS walks towards the window and picks up a photo frame with APRIL's photo in it. He looks at it like a lover until APRIL returns with JEREMY.

APRIL: Jeremy, you don't know my good friend Louis. He's been away all summer.

JEREMY: No. I have heard of you, but we've never met.

LOUIS: *[Offering his hand]* It's good to meet you.

JEREMY: Thanks. You too.

APRIL: Jeremy is doing a PhD at Melbourne.

LOUIS: Really! What in?

JEREMY: Politics, but really philosophy.

LOUIS: I understand.

APRIL: Louis is in politics, Jeremy. But you should know that, shouldn't you?

JEREMY: I probably should.

LOUIS: No, you shouldn't, Jeremy. My part of politics is the part you're not supposed know anything about, and it doesn't really have much to do with philosophy.

JEREMY: I won't ask any questions about it then.

LOUIS: Very wise.

APRIL: Shall we have a drink?

JEREMY: Thanks. But I had better be getting up to Ted. Is he upstairs?

APRIL: He's in his room. Come and see me before you go.

JEREMY: I will. Thanks. *[To LOUIS]* Nice to meet you.

LOUIS: You too.

JEREMY exits. APRIL and LOUIS sit and don't speak for a moment. Now she too is lost in thought.

APRIL: So? What do you think of him?

LOUIS: Oh, he's fine. He's very polite. Confident. I can see why you like him.

Act I - Scene I

APRIL: I can see you two hitting it off. In fact, he reminds me of you when we first met.

LOUIS: Hang on. That was only seven years ago. How old is he?

APRIL: He's only twenty-five, but he's quite mature and sensitive for his age.

LOUIS: You mean serious?

APRIL: When I met you, you were just a little boyish for a man of thirty-five. I don't mean you were immature. You were so passionate and enthusiastic about what you were doing. I could definitely see the remnants of that ardent, young twenty-five-year-old you must have been. There was still something vulnerable about you.

LOUIS: And now I am burnt-out and cynical.

APRIL: A little. And Jeremy is just a little too serious. It would do you both the world of good if I had you round to dinner every now and again. In fact, we should make this boy our new project.

LOUIS: What do you mean our new project?

APRIL: Well, you are always trying to get me involved in something or other.

LOUIS: Yeah. And I never succeed.

APRIL: Well here's something we can do. Let's take this boy in hand and help him a bit. You know all sorts of people in politics and he'll never get a job on his own, especially with a PhD in some obscure branch of political science.

LOUIS: Philosophy actually.

APRIL: Exactly. I can find him some money until he finishes his doctorate and then you can stitch him up with a job in government. We can't leave him at the mercy of that politics department. He'll end up stuck away in some dingy little office somewhere and they'll have him teaching Foucault before you can say soixante-neuf.

LOUIS: Don't be stupid. By the look of him that's exactly what he wants, or thinks he wants. They don't do a PhD if they want to go into politics.

APRIL: What do they do?

LOUIS: Law of course: industrial or corporate.

APRIL: Which is left and which is right?

LOUIS: It doesn't matter. It's only about who is paying you. Besides, I don't think that anyone going into politics now really bothers themselves with crude political distinctions like left and right.

We hear the front door open and someone entering.

Act I - Scene I

APRIL: *[Calling]* Is that you May? We're in here.

MAY enters.

MAY: *[Not seeing LOUIS]* Hello. *[Then seeing him]* Louis! I haven't seen you in ages.

LOUIS: I've been away for a month.

MAY: We've missed you.

LOUIS: Thanks. Not really?

MAY: Actually, I haven't. But I think April has. You see, she is so responsible all the time. It's only when you are around that she feels she's allowed to be frivolous. You have been away, what was it, a month? That's exactly the amount of time since April had any fun around here. With Teddy and his tutoring and me and my VCE, we've been a frivolity free household. *[She sits on the arm of the chair close to APRIL]* Isn't that right?

APRIL: It's impertinent but probably true. I just don't have old friends any more to relax with. You can only be completely frivolous with someone if you have known them for at least seven years?

LOUIS: I have never known you to be particularly frivolous.

MAY: She's not like that with you, of course. It's just when she comes home from one of your long lunches or after you have been here for dinner. She becomes all natty and girly and young, and we all get the feeling she is about to take off and start exploring alternative lifestyles.

LOUIS: Lucky you. All I get when I am with her is all the dull stuff about you kids and your boring extracurricular activities. I'm the one who has to provide the entertainment.

APRIL: There's no use pretending anymore Louis. She'll have to know sometime. Louis and I are having a raging affair and we never stop having passionate sex.

MAY: Well, Louis doesn't seem to think it's so passionate if all you talk about is me and Teddy and Saturday morning Kanga Cricket.

APRIL: That's just it. When you have a bit on the side, it's disrespectful to your husband if you don't at least save all the good conversational topics for him. If Louis wants the good sex, he can't have everything.

LOUIS: Do I get a choice?

APRIL: No.

MAY: Well I am going upstairs before this becomes completely gross. Is Teddy up there?

APRIL: Yes, he's with Jeremy.

MAY: Is Jeremy here? Good. I want to talk to him about what subjects to avoid.

LOUIS: Yes, St Jeremy is here like a long hot summer.

MAY: I knew you would like him! [Leaving] He's a little bit hot and sweaty and far too brainy, but he's useful. Some experienced woman needs to take him in hand and organise his sex life though. He was probably a real dork at school and then got a little bit cooler at uni where being a geek wasn't totally frowned on. I could possibly organise his social life for him, I suppose. At least get him out of those clothes!

Exit MAY.

APRIL: Actually. I wonder how she would go living on campus?

Scene Two:

We are as in scene one, only much later that afternoon. APRIL is sitting reading. After some time, obviously waiting for JEREMY, she remembers that she has to plan her week. She makes the following list out aloud. It is in rhyming verse, but should not be recited as such. She is saying it to herself and only the audience should perceive that it is verse.

APRIL: Monday morning is piano lessons,
Monday afternoon – choir.
Tuesday is before school swimming
And Wednesday is project day...
[Recalling the topic] 'Fire'.
Thursday after school Kids' Club,
And my gym class, of course.
Friday he was going to Mia's house,
That's off – she fell off her horse.
So Friday is now empty,
But not a second of the weekend is free.
So what will we do on Friday?
Mental Note!
Make time for Teddy and me.

JEREMY enters.

JEREMY: We have just finished.

APRIL: How is he going?

JEREMY: Really well. He's such a clever kid. You know you really don't need me at all.

APRIL: So you really like him, Jeremy?

JEREMY: Yeah. I do. He's a really nice boy. You've brought him up so well.

APRIL: That's marvellous, because he thinks the world of you. He really looks up to you. I think he feels safe with you. Before you came, I was so worried about him. He wasn't happy at school and he didn't seem to really mix with the other children. Now everything seems to be fitting in perfectly. You've done a fantastic job. I can't thank you enough.

JEREMY: It's probably nothing to do with me. Some kids just take a little time to find their feet at school. I don't think I ever really felt happy with school til I went to uni.

APRIL: We've never really talked, Jeremy. Just you and me. Do you have time now? How about a glass of wine?

JEREMY: Thanks. That would be lovely.

APRIL: *[Pouring the wine]* Come and sit down. Do you know what the population of Bogota is?

JEREMY: No idea. Why? *[Taking the glass]* Thank you.

APRIL: Don't worry. It's odd when you think about it. I don't really know you at all. Conrad and I are paying you to tutor Teddy, you've been living with us practically all summer and

Act 1 - Scene 2

we've been chatting away, but I don't know anything about you. I know your CV and your referees told me how brilliant you are, but that doesn't really tell me anything I haven't found out myself. Who are you, Jeremy?

JEREMY: That's quite difficult to answer, actually. No one ever really asks you about who you are or what you think. People are usually more interested in what you do. When you are a student, you don't actually do much. I don't know. I could tell you what three things I have in my fridge now.

APRIL: I'm sorry. I didn't mean to put you on the spot. And I certainly don't want to know anything as personal as what you've got in your fridge. Tell me about your parents.

JEREMY: Well, actually, that is quite personal, because I don't have any.

APRIL: Oh God. I'm so stupid...

JEREMY: No. I'm really sorry. It's fine. But, you know, when someone asks you that question, in my position, there's really no way to answer it without a little bit of melodrama. It was a long time ago, it was fairly short and painless and, I would have to say that when I think about it, it didn't really wreck my life. It's horrible, but it's a fact. In my experience, we only really get freaked out by the things we can't quite put our fingers on.

APRIL: That's true.

JEREMY: The problem is, when your parents die, it becomes the great fact, the great event of your life. Everything else you do or think seems to most people to be pretty dull. And, to be honest, I think once your parents are gone, whatever age you are, life can seem a little pointless. Unless you are one of those political types who has to go out and become US president to prove to their dead father that they could actually do it. I love those guys. I wish I could do that kind of thing. To me, there's no one around to prove anything to, so what's the point?

APRIL: Except that it hasn't stopped you doing things. All that writing and research you do seems extraordinary. When I first spoke to your supervisor he told me how prolific you are. You must show me what you've written.

JEREMY: But that's the thing. I don't show anyone and I just publish my work in really respectable journals because they are the ones that no one actually reads. I don't do it because I am shy. I do it because I am really quite arrogant. I don't want to be rude, and I am not talking about you, but I don't show my stuff because I know it's good and nothing anyone can say to me really makes me feel anything at all.

APRIL: Perhaps that is what it was all for – the great event?

JEREMY: What do you mean?

APRIL: Do you ever wonder why your parents died?

Act 1 - Scene 2

JEREMY: You mean, do I think there is meaning in the universe?

APRIL: Not really. I was just thinking that with your attitude towards your work you might be tempted to think of your life in more positive terms?

JEREMY: What would they be?

APRIL: It's a gloomy picture you're painting for the rest of us – ninety percent of the population running around working, playing, singing, dancing just to impress their parents. Perhaps your way is the only purely unselfconscious way? There must be a certain satisfaction in thinking that the only reason for doing something is the thing itself.

JEREMY: Maybe. Do you have anyone to impress?

APRIL: According to your rule, I must have. My parents are in place and my little family is coming along nicely, plenty of scope to set out to impress.

JEREMY: Lucky you.

APRIL: Except that I don't feel any inclination to impress anyone in any way.

JEREMY: So you have a full house but nothing to give the audience?

APRIL: Apparently.

JEREMY: What would you say to the audience if you had to?

APRIL: It would be short. I'd say that my parents didn't fuck me up, like Philip Larkin said, that I had a happy childhood. I'd say that I never really needed anything I couldn't get, that no one ever hurt me, no one ever deceived me and that, as far as I know, I never really hurt anyone else.

JEREMY: But you wouldn't say the one thing that really frightens you.

APRIL: What's that?

JEREMY: *[Touching her hand]* That you have never really felt safe once in your life.

They say nothing for a minute. Just looking at his hand on hers. April does not abhor this, but she says:

APRIL: You should probably go.

He stands up.

JEREMY: I will. Goodbye.

APRIL: Good night.

Jeremy exits. APRIL is left sitting on the couch. We hear JEREMY open and close the door behind him.

Scene Three:

The scene is set as in scenes one and two. It is just after nine the next morning. LOUIS is sitting on the couch waiting nervously for APRIL. There are takeaway coffees and pastry things on the coffee table. LOUIS is preparing a speech he plans to make to APRIL, but never will.

LOUIS: April I've got to tell you something.
No, April when I was away. No.
April, where do you see this going?
No, April I've been talking to May.
You know exactly what I am feeling.
Come on, we know each other better than that?
Surely we owe ourselves happiness
Before we get old – and fat.
April what are we going to tell Conrad?
Perhaps we should put it back on the shelf!
April what on earth are we going to do?
My God! I'm talking to myself.

We hear the door open and close and APRIL enters.

APRIL: Hello. What are you doing here so early? I just dropped Teddy off.

LOUIS: I have been up all night, must be jetlag. I drove past quite late last night, but all the lights were out, so I came back early, with pastries!

APRIL: Are you stalking me?

LOUIS: I wanted to talk to you.

APRIL: Sounds serious. I'm glad you didn't come last night. I wasn't really in a fit state for serious talk.

LOUIS: May's right. The second I go you do get all frivolous.

APRIL: Not exactly. I had a long talk with Jeremy after he finished with Teddy. You know his parents are both dead and he's really quite philosophical about the whole thing. He's obviously terribly hurt. He seems to have, I don't know, closed in. He's marvellous with Teddy – very giving. But he doesn't seem to have any needs of his own. It's almost as if he is impervious to receiving anything – or at least he thinks he is.

LOUIS: That's a challenge for any mother. But it's unlikely that he doesn't need anything. He's probably just not quite sure how to articulate what he wants.

APRIL: Sometimes I think that it's only people who have suffered that have a right to want things.

LOUIS: That is pretty much everyone, though.

Act 1 - Scene 3

APRIL: But that is just it. That is what I was so devastated about last night when I was talking with Jeremy. I realised that I have never suffered anything.

LOUIS: Except fools gladly! [Pleased with his gag] That's nonsense. You just think you haven't. We all start suffering the minute we are born.

APRIL: What, for example? What have I suffered?

LOUIS: I haven't given it much thought. It can't be all roses living with Conrad, much as we love him. What about when Carol died?

APRIL: I was upset and I miss her, but I'm not sure I would call that suffering. In my life, it's May who does the suffering. Now perhaps it's Jeremy too. You see what I am doing? I am surrounding myself with suffering and insecurity and I am living off it.

LOUIS: Did you ever lose anyone?

APRIL: Not that I know of.

LOUIS: There's nothing you wanted that you couldn't have?

APRIL: No.

LOUIS: No one?

APRIL is awkward and annoyed at the direction the conversation has gone.

APRIL: No one at all.

LOUIS: Then I feel sorry for you. Because either what you say is true or you are so dead inside that you can't even register any feelings of pain. You and Jeremy might make a good couple.

APRIL: What great pain and loss do you feel that makes you so alive?

LOUIS: "I am alone, a bachelor and the night is upon me" or at least the afternoon is upon me, which is much worse.

APRIL: So what do people who suffer do about it?

LOUIS: They fall in love.

APRIL: So who are you in love with?

There is a pause in the conversation.

LOUIS: I'm nuts about May.

APRIL: May? She's half your age.

LOUIS: You say that like it's a bad thing.

APRIL: It's off.

LOUIS: I don't see why. If I were a rich, ageing media magnate you would think it was quite normal. In fact I think it would be a very good arrangement. She's a poor penniless orphan living with a mean and begrudging foster mother, I have nothing to spend my money

Act 1 - Scene 3

             on, and I'm not getting any younger. Yes. I think it could be a very tidy arrangement indeed.

APRIL: Except that it's totally disgusting, and she probably thinks you're old enough to be her grandfather.

We can hear the door opening and MAY and another person are about to enter.

LOUIS: Is that her? Let's ask her now shall we?

MAY enters with JEREMY much to APRIL's astonishment.

MAY: I found Jeremy at uni, so I made him drive me back.

LOUIS: May, are you particularly busy at the moment?

MAY is looking in her bag.

MAY: Not particularly.

LOUIS: Well what would you say to us getting married?

MAY: Fine with me. As long as we get the pre-nup sorted.

LOUIS: And you wouldn't think it disgusting to be married to an old guy like me?

MAY: Not if the money's right.

LOUIS: *[To APRIL]* Thank you. On that triumphant note I'm leaving.

JEREMY: I'd better be getting back to uni too. Bye.

MAY: Thanks for the lift, Jeremy.

JEREMY: No worries.

MAY: Louis, you will be hearing from my lawyer!

LOUIS: Good.

APRIL: Are we seeing you this afternoon, Jeremy?

JEREMY: Of course.

LOUIS: *[Kissing APRIL patronisingly on the top of her head as he passes behind her]* Goodbye darling.

APRIL: Bye, dirty old man.

LOUIS and JEREMY exit. MAY slumps down into the couch.

MAY: So I have to do some stupid thing called 'Plato to NATO', which I think is really just politics, and I have decided to do French, English and Cinema Studies. Not exactly inspiring, but it will do.

APRIL: You and Louis have an amusing little banter going there.

Act 1 - Scene 3

MAY: Yeah. He's pretty funny.

APRIL: Not as funny as he used to be. He's become more serious with age.

MAY: I haven't known him that long.

APRIL: Did you notice how he just kissed me then? He hasn't done that for years. It was quite a shock in a way. In fact it was a strange morning altogether.

MAY: What do you mean?

APRIL: It is unusual for him to drop round so early. He said he wanted to talk to me and we ended up having something that felt a little bit like a fight.

MAY: What about?

APRIL: It wasn't really anything. It just seemed like something clicked somewhere and it suddenly got nasty.

MAY: Can't have been too nasty if he gave you a kiss on the way out.

APRIL: You don't know Louis. He abominates air kissing. It's probably something to do with his French background. Anyway tell me about Jeremy.

MAY: What do you mean?

APRIL: Don't you think he's fantastic? Teddy is crazy about him.

MAY: Well, I wouldn't go as far as that. But he's pretty cool.

APRIL: Bit old for you? Bit too brainy?

MAY: Not really. He's a bit arrogant though and really full of himself for a geek.

APRIL: Actually we talked about that a bit last night. In fact we had quite a chat. I can see how you might find him a bit self-satisfied and maybe a bit awkward, but I think he's quite a thoughtful boy. I like him a lot. He's sweet and sensitive.

MAY: He has his moments.

APRIL: I wonder if I just see him that way because I'm older, or whether people his own age appreciate him too?

MAY: I think he's got some friends he likes. They are probably not as crazy about him as you are though.

APRIL: *[Laughing]* Don't be silly. But why wouldn't his friends appreciate him?

MAY: I wouldn't say they don't appreciate him, I'd just say they probably don't think about it much. You are probably thinking about him more in terms of Teddy, and you feel grateful to him and relieved that Teddy's coming along so well.

APRIL: Do you think he's attractive?

MAY: You really are nuts about him, aren't you?

APRIL: No. I'm interested. I don't really know anyone one like Jeremy. I mean no one his age or who does what he does. I suppose I was surprised to find a boy like that so sympathetic. You're right. I am probably thinking about how Teddy will grow up and wondering if he'll end up a bit like Jeremy.

MAY: I don't think Jeremy's that special. I mean I don't think he's so different from a lot of other guys his age. I suppose Teddy might be a bit like that at that age.

APRIL: He seems to me to be quite attractive. I know he's probably a bit old for you, but do you think he's good looking?

MAY: I haven't thought about it. I don't really know him like that.

There is a lull in the conversation as MAY feels awkward and APRIL is somewhat lost in her own thoughts.

APRIL: May, I was thinking we never really discussed what you were going to do about your living arrangements when you left school.

MAY: No.

APRIL: Of course we want you to stay here as long as you like, you're part of the family obviously. We just never thought to ask you if you wanted to think about living in college or closer to campus.

MAY: Some of my friends are doing that, but college doesn't really sound very me. As well as the expense.

APRIL: That wouldn't be a problem if you did want to go. We could sort it out. But it sounds like you would rather stay here with us for a while.

MAY: Yes. If that's all right. I am thinking about getting a job and I would like to start paying board. You have been so generous over the years...

APRIL: There's no need for that. There's always room for you here and we love having you so much. I don't want you to think about paying us anything, particularly while you are a student.

MAY: Perhaps we should think about it! But that's very good of you.

APRIL: *[Hugging her and tearing up slightly]* Oh May. *[They hug for a while and then have that difficult moment in breaking away. APRIL wipes a tear]* Well, I suppose you could always get Louis to be your protector if Conrad's portfolio takes a dive in some sudden international financial crisis. *[They laugh]*

MAY: Do you think he would set me up in a posh flat if I let him?

Act 1 - Scene 3

APRIL: Dress allowance, flowers, chocolates and all! He'd like that.

MAY: Sounds like Gigi. *[She sings in a French accent]* "Thank Heaven, for little girls. They grow up in the most delightful way!"

APRIL: Maurice Chevalier. Yuk!

MAY: He's not that bad. Why didn't he ever get married?

APRIL: Maurice Chevalier? *[Knowing full well she means Louis]*

MAY: Louis.

APRIL: He had one or two quite big things before I met him. I think he was supposed to get married to a girl called Miranda, but it didn't work out. He has had a couple of things in the past few years but most of our age group are off the market. He says he goes largely ignored by women with children.

MAY: Did you two ever have a thing?

APRIL: No. I was with Conrad well before I met Louis. We've become very close over the years and we spend a lot of time together. I rely on him quite a bit when I think about it. Conrad is not exactly my soul mate.

MAY: Do you think Louis is?

APRIL: No. Don't misunderstand me. Conrad and I are very close, probably much closer than either of us cares to admit. In some ways, that kind of relationship, that closeness can be a little bit frightening. Perhaps that's where Louis comes in. Louis and I have much more in common than I do with Conrad, but you can only get so far with similar tastes in art and books and music.

MAY: Do you think Louis sees it that way?

APRIL: I'm sure he does. I suppose he's thought about it. I mean thought about us. I have. But, even if we did something about it, how would we start? If he kissed me I think I'd laugh.

MAY: That would probably kill the moment.

APRIL: Probably. Anyway, that's enough about my love life. I am a happily married woman. You should be telling me all about yours.

MAY: There's not a great deal to tell. You should know. They're not exactly beating down the front door or ringing the phone off the hook. I don't really have a lot of luck with boys. I think I'm a bit too loud and opinionated.

APRIL: There's nothing wrong with that.

MAY: It does tend to scare them off a little bit though.

APRIL: Only the weak willed, and you don't want to be bothered with them anyway.

Act 1 - Scene 3

MAY: I could afford to be bothered with a little bit of that, just to keep my eye in.

APRIL: But there must be heaps of boys interested in you. You're lovely! There's nothing fake or manufactured about you at all. I love the way you express yourself. You're so confident and forthright, and funny!

MAY: Stop it! I'm trying to get a boyfriend not a gig at the Comedy Festival.

APRIL: But what about sex? *[MAY is slightly taken aback]* Sorry, is that a conversation you don't really want to have?

MAY: No. It's just that…

APRIL: Should I have talked to you about this before?

MAY: I'm not sure what you mean.

APRIL: You and I have this unusual relationship. We are not mother and daughter, but we're not quite 'just friends'. I suppose I was thinking whether we should be talking about sex and… things.

MAY: You mean the birds and the bees?

APRIL: No. Of course not.

MAY: I can tell you anything you need to know. Married life is not always the best preparation for a girl!

APRIL: *[Laughing]* That's it. I am not talking to you about this at all.

MAY: Did you talk to your mother about sex and boys?

APRIL: No, of course not.

MAY: There it is then. Besides, there has only really been one major... incident. And nothing really came of it.

APRIL: Do you want to tell me about it?

MAY: It was New Year's Eve, on the beach at Portsea.

APRIL: This year? Who was it?

MAY: Nothing came of it. It was just a one-night thing.

APRIL: Did you want to see him again?

MAY: I don't know. He's nice. But I was a bit surprised that nothing came of it.

APRIL: Did we meet him? We were there for a while.

MAY: I don't really want to get into who he is.

APRIL: It wasn't Jeremy?

MAY: Look nothing came of it. Perhaps we should just leave it.

APRIL: But why didn't you want to tell me?

Act 1 - Scene 3

MAY: You are very keen on him. He works for you. It just didn't feel right.

APRIL: But you see him all the time. You were just with him. What does he say about it?

MAY: We never really talked about it.

APRIL: Never?

MAY: No. It was awkward the next morning and physically he was a bit prickly, so I just left it. I didn't talk to him about it. Then a few days passed and when I saw him he was fine and really quite friendly. We just never got to talk about it. We kind of got into this big brother, little sister thing. I boss him about a bit and he acts as if he's my lap dog and that is about it.

APRIL: That's terrible. You must be really hurt! He could have at least talked to you about it.

MAY: It's not as bad as that. It was just a difficult situation. It's probably not all his fault.

APRIL: That's all very convenient for him! I can't believe he would do that! That's outrageous behaviour. I'm really annoyed. I'm not having him here with Teddy if he can't even be honest with you about a thing like this.

MAY: April it's not that big a deal, don't worry. I'm not upset about it. He didn't hurt me. We're fine. It's just like we skipped the difficult bit.

APRIL: Well, I feel like I should talk to him about it. I'm responsible. I didn't have him in the house so that he could play around with you.

MAY: Please don't talk to him about it. It would be terribly embarrassing.

APRIL: Well, I'm not going to have him here if he's going to do this kind of thing.

MAY: But Teddy needs him and you know how important that is. You were the one who was so impressed with him. None of that has changed. You'll calm down a bit and you'll realise that it's not really a big deal.

APRIL: I am just so disappointed with him. That is not the way to behave. I really feel like he's let me down.

MAY: *[Comforting APRIL]* It's fine. There's really nothing to be worried about.

Scene Four:

It is later that afternoon. May is sitting in a bar waiting for someone. The ambient bar music stops and we can hear May singing under her breath.

MAY: Some day I'll find a boy
With an open mind
And an outlook on life so mature,
That I'll count up to three
And he'll know that it's me
And our love, life and happiness secure.
Just one glance at his face,
Will all sadness erase
And the pain of the past will be gone.
When he sits by my side
My head's gone with the tide
And our love it goes on and on.

The ambient music returns and Louis arrives and sits.

MAY: Did you have a fight with April today?

LOUIS: Does she say we did?

MAY: She thought you might have.

LOUIS: It wasn't a fight. I just snapped at her a little bit. She's not used to it.

MAY: What about?

LOUIS: Nothing much. I wanted to talk to her, and she just kept crapping on about Jeremy Brightwell. Which is annoying.

MAY: Are you in love with her?

LOUIS: In what sense?

MAY: You know what sense.

LOUIS: Let's see. I think about her all the time and when I'm not thinking about her, I remind myself to think about her. So I suppose I must be.

MAY: That can't be easy.

LOUIS: It's not. It's been a long time. Intermittently broken up by a thing with someone here or there. But somehow I always end up back with April.

MAY: I think she knows that. But I don't think she's smug about it, if that is any consolation to you.

LOUIS: You're right. She's not smug. She is just a little tired of it and more easily distracted than I am. Which explains Jeremy Brightwell.

MAY: We had a fight today.

LOUIS: You and April? What about?

Act 1 - Scene 4

MAY: We had that long overdue sex talk, and she wormed it out of me that Jeremy and I had a thing on New Year's Eve.

LOUIS: Really? You and Jeremy? Poor April. That would have hurt.

MAY: She was upset. Now she's threatening to dump him. After all that about what a star he is, it's a bit awkward.

LOUIS: In a woman like April, I'm not sure if jealousy or hypocrisy is worse.

MAY: How will she explain it to Conrad?

LOUIS: She'll think of something. She's very good on her feet.

MAY: You mean she's experienced at this kind of thing?

LOUIS: Not that I know of. But Conrad is experienced at this kind of thing. He helps her a great deal.

MAY: I suppose when you are so busy running around helping everyone else you need someone to look after you.

LOUIS: Particularly when you are a little lacking in self-examination.

MAY: She needs to do a little more of that, doesn't she? It would get the rest of us off the hook.

LOUIS: Do you find it difficult living with April?

MAY: I don't want to sound – what's the word – churlish? April and Conrad really saved my life. When my mother died I was completely alone. They took me in and took over all her responsibilities, and more. I can't imagine what would have happened to me without them. But it's a strange relationship. Everything most people get from their parents and take for granted, I feel I have to be grateful for. I don't get that from April. In fact, she's never been that kind of parent to me. She doesn't nag me, we don't really fight, it's almost eerily cordial. Of course that all makes it worse and I feel I owe her even more. She's so good to me, so kind and giving, that I feel she owns me body and soul, like some sort of indentured slave.

LOUIS: So telling her about Jeremy felt like an act of defiance.

MAY: Yeah. I feel like I have betrayed her.

LOUIS: Maybe it's a good thing? I suspect the problem with your relationship is that it lacks a criminal element. Perhaps it's liberation day?

MAY: For her too. She raised the issue of my future plans, which she has never done before. There was no overt pressure about it but I just got a little feeling that she wants me out of the way.

LOUIS: I'm sure that's not true. Not really. I think she would be very sad if you weren't around, but she may feel that she needs a holiday, like you do.

Act 1 - Scene 4

MAY: Particularly while Jeremy's around.

LOUIS: Exactly.

MAY: I even had the feeling that she wanted to fob me off onto you.

LOUIS: That was my fault. And you didn't help the situation with all that stuff about pre-nups. She pretended to be grossed out by it but the way she is feeling at the moment any port in the storm will do. I was trying to make her jealous and, of course, she jumped on it. I wonder whether she really wants Jeremy or just wants to get rid of me?

MAY: That's what I was thinking too.

LOUIS: Anyway, as the criminal element has been unleashed and we have all betrayed each other, I think we should call this Liberation Day!

MAY: You haven't committed any crimes. What about a final act of liberation for you? You have a huge house, right near uni. Why don't you call April's bluff and let me come and be your housemate for a while? Rent free, of course.

LOUIS: As Julia Roberts says in *Notting Hill*, "Tempting but no."

Scene Five:

The scene returns to APRIL's veranda. APRIL is waiting for JEREMY in her sitting room. The doorbell rings, she exits to answer it and they both return.

APRIL: Teddy's gone to a friend's house and he won't be back 'til after dinner so we may as well forget about it for today. But I did want to talk to you about the future.

JEREMY: Right.

APRIL: Jeremy, Teddy is coming along really well, and we have talked about what a fantastic job you have done. I just think it's probably time we made a change. This is his last year before he goes to his new school and I think he could probably do with a little more freedom, just before things get really intense next year.

JEREMY: Sure. I did say that you don't really need me anymore.

APRIL: That's right. We'd love to keep having you and I know Teddy will miss you but I think it would also be good for him to row his own boat for a while and build up his confidence on his own.

JEREMY: There's definitely something in that.

APRIL: I know that you rely on the money to help you pay your way though the PhD, but I am sure you'll have no trouble getting more work. I'll help you there as much as I can.

JEREMY: That's fine. Actually this year I really need to write up my thesis and I was only keeping Teddy on because he's such a good kid and I really like coming here.

APRIL: We will all miss you. Hopefully we can catch up every now and then, have you over for dinner?

JEREMY: That would be lovely. I'd hate to lose contact.

APRIL: I am sure that won't happen. In fact would you like to come over on the weekend for lunch? It would give you a chance to talk to Teddy about it.

JEREMY: Great. Thanks. I may as well go and I'll see you on Sunday?

APRIL: Fine. Thanks for understanding. I didn't want to disappoint you. It just seemed best. Of course we'll pay you for the month.

JEREMY: *[Leaving]* Thanks. That would be helpful. *[Stopping]* April, can I just ask? This doesn't have anything to do with what happened the other day, does it?

APRIL: What do you mean?

Act I - Scene 5

JEREMY: I mean about that conversation we had. I felt we had a little moment there and now I am worried that it made you uncomfortable.

APRIL: That's not the reason I am stopping the tutoring.

JEREMY: No, of course. But it did make you feel uncomfortable.

APRIL: It did a bit.

JEREMY: I am sorry. Is there anything I can do about it? I'd hate to stop coming here just because of a misunderstanding between us. To be honest, I think we've become quite close. I would have to say that one of the reasons I have kept up the job is because of you. I know we haven't spent a great deal of time together, but I really enjoy when we do get a chance to talk. I know you are married and you are probably not interested in me in that way but even so.

APRIL: I didn't realise. I thought you were coming here because of May.

JEREMY: So you know about New Year's Eve?

APRIL: Yes. I was a bit shocked actually. I imagine she feels a bit hurt by it all.

JEREMY: She didn't give me that impression. I don't really think she's interested in me at all.

APRIL: I think you are being naïve.

JEREMY: She never said anything about it.

APRIL: She's so young. She finds it hard to talk to you.

JEREMY: That's a first. She's never had any problem expressing her views in the past.

APRIL: Now I know you are being naïve. It's true she puts up a confident front but you have to remember she's very young and almost totally inexperienced. I don't know what happened between you two but I know it was something. I would think she's feeling quite vulnerable at the moment, especially if you haven't talked to her about it and told her what you are thinking.

JEREMY: Are you annoyed at me, or something?

APRIL: What do you mean?

JEREMY: You said you were shocked about me and May. I was just wondering if you were angry with me too. Perhaps you feel I have let you down?

APRIL: It's really none of my business. I do feel protective of May.

JEREMY: But I am talking about the way you feel about me.

APRIL: What has that got to do with it? *[JEREMY kisses her and waits for a response.]* What did you do that for?

JEREMY: The discussion didn't seem to be going anywhere worthwhile.

APRIL: Is that the only reason?

JEREMY: No. I have been wanting to kiss you for ages.

She kisses him back and the lights go down.

Scene Six:

The same, sometime later.

APRIL: We shouldn't have done that.

JEREMY: I know. I feel terrible. I don't mean about you. I mean about being here in your house and about Conrad and Teddy, and May.

APRIL: Don't worry. No one is home. They won't find out.

JEREMY: Do you really think that I have upset May?

APRIL: You're thinking about that now?

JEREMY: We were talking about it.

APRIL: I think you had better go Jeremy.

JEREMY: I'm sorry. You're right. I was being naïve.

There is a noise at the front door. LOUIS and MAY are returning from the bar.

APRIL: We're in here!

JEREMY: *[Softly to APRIL]* I'm sorry.

APRIL: What have you two been doing? Did you elope?

LOUIS: We just went to a bar for a drink. She's eighteen now so it's all perfectly legal. What have you been doing?

APRIL: Jeremy has just dumped us for his PhD. He says he can't come to tutor Teddy anymore until he's Dr Brightwell.

LOUIS: That just means he wants you to pay him more.

JEREMY: No. I have decided it's finally time I put my head down and finished the thing.

APRIL: And he doesn't want the distraction of us!

MAY: Nonsense. He'll be back in a week.

LOUIS: No. He looks serious to me. Summer was bound to turn into autumn.

JEREMY: Actually I'll be back on the weekend for lunch.

LOUIS: That will definitely soften the blow.

JEREMY: I had better go. Otherwise we might all end up in tears.

LOUIS: Bye Jeremy. Good luck with your thesis.

JEREMY: Thanks. If it doesn't work out, I might have to lean on you for a job.

LOUIS: Good. I hope you do.

JEREMY: Bye everyone. Thanks April.

Act I - Scene 6

APRIL is busying herself and does not respond.

MAY: I'll see you out.

Exit MAY and JEREMY

LOUIS: That was awkward.

APRIL: What do you mean?

LOUIS: Something was obviously happening between you two when we walked in.

APRIL: Well, I don't want to discuss it.

LOUIS pauses a minute as he looks out the window. APRIL is cleaning up.

LOUIS: April I'm sorry.

APRIL: What for?

LOUIS: For whatever part I am playing in messing up your life. You know the way I feel about you. I have never said anything to you because I have deluded myself that I was doing you a big favour. You are married to Conrad and you have Teddy and May. I suppose I thought that if I never told you what I was feeling then you would never really have to deal with the problem. The thing is, you are probably dealing with it anyway. Obviously you are not devastated by an unconsummated passion, I'm not that deluded, but I think I know you well enough to say that there is something between us. Anyway, whatever is or isn't between us, it certainly would not have helped things if I had come out with some sort of fumbling declaration.

APRIL: So why do it now?

LOUIS: I know. I'm sorry about Jeremy. I think we both know he's not the great love of your life but, as soon as I got back, I could see how important he was to you.

APRIL: I know . . . but. [Pause] So where does that leave you and me?

LOUIS: I think we blew it.

APRIL: You are right. Did you really think it was ever going to work?

LOUIS: Not without a certain degree of selfishness and probably a fair bit of deception. You see, I gave up the idea of us being together years ago. What I tried to hold on to was a little piece of you. I just wanted to be part of your life. Once a week, once a month, ten times a year, perhaps. Just to feel that in a whole year of distractions, we had at least one particular moment for ourselves.

APRIL: It sounds ridiculously simple when you put it like that.

LOUIS: It does. But when you think about it, we've probably only had about two hours of real conversation in the last year.

Act 1 - Scene 6

APRIL: You are right.

LOUIS: But you are not thinking about that now. You're thinking about Jeremy and about May and how the Hell it all got so mixed up.

APRIL: Perhaps I am. To be honest, I'm just so tired. I can't think.

LOUIS: Which is why this little episode in the April and Louis story has probably been a huge waste of time. Perhaps when you wake up in the morning, you'll have forgotten all about it. Anyway, I'm going.

APRIL: Will we catch up soon?

LOUIS: I'll tell you a secret April. Almost once a year I promise myself that I am going to dump you and never see you again.

APRIL: So what happens?

LOUIS: You never call me.

LOUIS exits. APRIL is exhausted. She sits down on the couch and bursts into tears. Soon MAY returns.

MAY: April! What's the matter?

APRIL: It's nothing really. I'm just so tired.

MAY: You are tired. It's because you are such a worker and you look after everyone. It's time we started looking after you.

APRIL:	I can look after myself. I've done a pretty good job of it over the last few days.
MAY:	Yeah and you're a mess.
APRIL:	You're just such a comforting little thing aren't you?
MAY:	Jeremy's gone.
APRIL:	Louis has too.
MAY:	What on Earth do these men want?
APRIL:	*[Laughing]* I don't know and I don't care. Whatever it is, it is sure to be something different in five minutes anyway.
MAY:	They never say what they want.
APRIL:	And when they do, they never mean what they say. *[They laugh and embrace]* I used to talk to your mum like this.
MAY:	Really?
APRIL:	Yeah. We'd have a terrible fight, usually about some boy, and then one of us would remember that we didn't really care anyway, and that our friendship was all that really mattered.
MAY:	Was that when you were at school?
APRIL:	School and beyond.

Act I - Scene 6

MAY: Really? You two must have been terribly worried about nabbing a man.

APRIL: It wasn't like that at all. In fact, at that age, we probably thought men would just come up with the rations.

MAY: Did you fight over Conrad? Or my father?

APRIL: No one could ever really fight over Conrad. He's the sort of man that lets everyone know exactly where they stand.

MAY: What about my father?

APRIL: I never met him. It was a fairly brief thing between them. Carol kept him at a distance and then he went off. I suppose, in a way, we did fight about him. After he left, she told me a little bit of what happened and, when I think back, the whole thing really upset me. He was probably quite normal, but then it all sounded so dangerous and threatening that I became really angry with her. We had our usual scrap about it, but then nobody stopped to say how stupid it was and we never really got past it.

MAY: When did you resolve it?

APRIL: We didn't.

MAY: But how did you come to have me?

APRIL: It just happened that way. Carol and I weren't talking, but we knew where to find each other if we had to. You can hardly avoid that in

Melbourne. Anyway, when she died a group of us who knew her well got together and I got the prize.

MAY: That's not how I understood it at all.

APRIL: Well, I don't think it was really like that anyway. Carol and I had been friends for so long, it wasn't as if those five years were so important. We were both so busy with other things. At that time of life, it's quite good to have a real excuse for not keeping in touch. Most people just drift apart casually.

MAY: So you never even discussed me coming to live with you.

APRIL: No, we didn't have the chance. I think she would have wanted it this way though, given the circumstances. I would have wanted my daughter to live with her if I had been in her position. It's easy to have a long-term dispute. Not so easy to wipe out twenty-five years of friendship.

MAY: So you never got to resolve it with her?

APRIL: I didn't get to speak to her before she died, if that's what you mean.

MAY: Didn't you want to?

APRIL: I don't think either of us cared about the fight. I knew she was ill, and I rang the hospital, but they told me she didn't want to see anyone.

Act I - Scene 6

MAY: But I am sure if you had turned up she would have seen you.

APRIL: Frankly, I was relieved. I didn't want to see her at that point, it would have been too disturbing.

MAY: But you never got to speak to her again.

APRIL: Perhaps when you are that close with someone it doesn't matter. I knew so much about her. I think I understood her very well. I know why she didn't want us there at the end.

MAY: Do you miss her?

APRIL: Every day.

MAY puts her arm around APRIL.

MAY: Did we have a fight?

APRIL: Perhaps a misunderstanding. I'm so glad you are here.

MAY: So am I.

APRIL: I don't want you to live anywhere else for a while.

MAY: I'm not going to.

APRIL: So what do we do about Jeremy?

MAY: I've had enough of Jeremy. I told him to bugger off. So I wouldn't be expecting him for lunch on Sunday.

APRIL: Really? We'll never get rid of him now.

Curtain

www.ingramcontent.com/pod-product-compliance
Lightning Source LLC
Chambersburg PA
CBHW071320080526
44587CB00018B/3290